Starting a
Podcast

10 Proven Steps to Creating Your First
Successful Podcast

Jerry Kershen

© 2016

TABLE OF CONTENTS

INTRODUCTION

Have you ever wanted to make a career or at least start a hobby as a podcaster but have just never gotten around to it? If so, you've come to the right place. This e-book is going to go over the 10 biggest steps towards making your dream of starting your own podcasts become a reality.

Just so we're all on the same page, podcasting is a type of digital media mostly in the form of either video or audio that is presented as an episodic series; subscribers or followers of the podcast can then download the podcast episodes individually or stream them online in order to watch or listen to them on their electronic device.

Today, there are many people who are able to gain thousands, and in some cases millions, of subscribers and viewers/listeners to their podcasts. But they didn't just wake up one day and decide to become a professional podcaster. They learned how to become successful at podcasting and creating informative and/or entertaining content largely via a trial and error process or by knowing the basic steps to ensuring a successful podcasting venture.

If you want to, you can quit reading this e-book now and go out and start podcasting this very moment. This means that you'll largely go through that trial and error process where you make mistakes, correct them, and then continue to make more mistakes and correcting them until eventually you figure out how to podcast effectively and gain a large enough audience. However, this is the long and frustrating route to becoming a successful podcaster, and it could end in failure for you if you grow weary or disheartened at your lack of progress.

If you would rather get into podcasting by knowing the basic steps, then you need to continue reading this e-book. We're going to cover everything you need to know about podcasting from what podcasting is to how you can ensure that you continue to be successful at it after you have already become successful.

In between those two things, we'll also learn about how to create content that is simultaneously engaging, creative, and informative, how to publish and distribute that content, and how to gain an initial dedicated audience for that content.

Podcasting manages to bring together the internet, a portable media player, audio, video, and entertainment together in a unique way that can reach out to audience you otherwise wouldn't have been able to reach out to. If you have a story to tell, information or knowledge to share with the world, fun skits or jokes to entertain people with (or a combination of those things), podcasting provides you with a unique and effective opportunity to do those things.

But you'll only be able to become successful at podcasting if you do it right, which is why each of the ten steps that we will go over is vitally important.

Let's get started.

STEP 1: WHAT IS PODCASTING?

You won't be able to become successful at podcasting if you don't first know what it is. Or maybe you think you know what podcasting is, but aren't entirely sure. Regardless of whether you're completely familiar with podcasting or not, this step is still important in order to ensure that we're all on the same page as to what podcasting is defined and what its capabilities and limitations are.

All that a podcast is, in its most basic form, is a digital media file that is produced in the form of a series. Usually a podcast will be audio, but it can also be video as well. People can then subscribe to a series of podcasts, and once they subscribe, they will then be updated as to when a new podcast is uploaded it. The podcast is then downloaded onto the subscriber's computer or music player, and they can listen to it whenever and wherever they desire.

The biggest difference between podcasting and radio or TV is that people have the ability to choose what they want to watch or listen to. If you tune into the radio or flick on the TV stations, you can only watch from the available channels there are, but there are even more specialized topics covered with podcasts, giving you a virtually unlimited number of podcasts to choose from. What's more is that the overwhelming majority of the time there are also multiple different podcasts on the same subject to choose from.

Listening to or watching a podcast is also significantly more convenient than watching TV or listening to the radio. With TV or radio, you can only watch or listen to it by the time the station sets for a particular program. With a podcast, once it's downloaded you can listen to it or watch it wherever and whenever you want, or listen to bits and pieces of it over the course of a day.

Long story short, if you have information that you want to share with the world and want to get that information out to as many people as possible, podcasting is an excellent opportunity for you to do so. Once you clearly define the topic of your podcast, people who are interested in that topic will seek you out and subscribe. There are also marketing techniques that you can use to draw people into your podcasts, which we'll cover later in this e-book.

Podcasting has become so prominent and powerful that it's built entire online communities. Podcasters will build communities around their shows and request comments or feedback. People can then set up blogs or forums on a particular podcast in order to communicate with other subscribers and listeners/viewers.

So in a nutshell, that's what podcasting is. But now the next question comes: why should you podcast?

STEP 2: WHY SHOULD YOU PODCAST?

As we have touched on already in this e-book, podcasting provides you with a very unique and yet powerful opportunity to share your voice, thoughts, and knowledge with the world. It doesn't matter whether you're running a business or are just into podcasting as a hobby. If you feel your voice needs to be heard, you definitely need to look into podcasting.

So regardless of whether you want to promote a product or service of yours, talk about whatever interests you, or essentially start your own talk show, there are many other reasons for why you would want to start and run a podcast as well. Let's go down the list and talk about what some of the most compelling of these reasons are:

IT'S FAST AND CHEAP

You will quickly find that it is very inexpensive to start and run a podcast. As long as you have equipment such as a computer, a microphone, and internet connection, you're practically set when it comes to cost.

And not only is podcasting dirt cheap, it's very fast. If you think that podcasting means that you'll be exclusively planning out an episode, recording multiple versions of it, spending countless hours editing it, and then maybe uploading it sometime next week, you're sorely mistaken. Once you get the hang of things, it's very much possible to have a podcast recorded and uploaded in just a few hours at the most.

It's certainly a faster and cheaper way to share your voice with the world versus doing something such as starting a YouTube Channel.

YOU CAN GAIN AN AUDIENCE FAST

As long as your content is good, you can gain an audience very fast. Not only will you gain an audience fast, but you'll be gaining an audience from all over the world as well. Don't be mistaken into believing that the audience from your podcast will be from a specific area (though they may be from a specific demographic). You can gain an incredibly focused audience from all corners of the world.

YOU ARE IN COMPLETE CONTROL OF YOUR PODCAST

Another beauty of podcasting is that you are in complete control of it. You determine how many podcasts casts you want to publish, how long each podcast is, the specific content of each podcast, the format of your podcast, where you want to record the podcast, and so on.

With podcasting, you don't have to submit to the rules of an authority (other than FCC regulations and copyright laws that you will have to abide by, of course). Instead, you are your own authority, and the only thing that limits what you can put out there is your creativity and your imagination.

IT'S PERSONAL

Since your podcast is your own and you are in total and complete control of it, this means that your podcasts are completely personal. Every human voice is unique, including your own. Your audience will soon be able to distinguish you from other people including those in your same niche. As a result, they will soon be able to connect with you via your podcast. This type of a relationship is not only very important for holding onto your audience and making them want to come back for more, but it's also vitally important for spreading the word about your podcast and reaching out to potentially new audience members.

You may also find that you will learn more about yourself via your podcasts. If you go back and listen to your podcasts once they are uploaded, or even if you just listen to portions of them, you will be able to identify specific things either in your voice or what you say that makes you you, which can always build your self-esteem regardless of how highly or how lowly you think of yourself.

IT'S AN OPPORTUNITY TO MAKE MONEY

Finally, if your podcast becomes successful enough, there is an opportunity for you to make a little extra cash on the side. Let's put it this way: if your content is valuable or entertaining, people will pay for it.

If you want to possibly make money with your podcast, what's important is that the niche of your content is clear and that it's oriented to a specific market. What's more, is your information needs to help those within that market as well.

Let's say that the subject of your podcast is on how to find ways to increase profits for small businesses. Small business owners from all over the country, if not the world, would gladly pay you for that information if they felt it was valuable or would help them actually increase profits.

This is why some podcasters don't offer their podcasts for free. They'll sell each episode for 99 cents or an entire season of episodes in a bundle for a reduced price and people will pay for it.

But make no mistake, you should never start selling your podcasts right off the bat. You should only set a price for each podcast episode once you've established yourself, built your reputation, have a large enough and focused audience, and an effective marketing strategy in place so you can reach out to advertisers to further expand your name and brand. You need to clearly prove that you can improve the life of your subscribers and listeners, or else they won't feel compelled enough to pay the dollar per episode that you may charge for them.

What's more, your podcasts need to be long enough as well. Even if your information is valuable and helpful, is somebody really going to pay a dollar for five or so minutes of content? Probably not. That's why almost all podcasts that are sold rather than offered for free run anywhere from 30 minutes to an hour. Then, once they've bought and downloaded it, listeners can tune into your podcast whenever they want to throughout the day.

STEP 3: PLANNING OUT YOUR PODCAST

The fact of the matter is that you will only be able to start running a podcast once you know full well what podcasting is inside and out, and once you know why you want to podcast.

Once you have determined that podcasting is something you want to pursue and you are willing to set aside the time and resources necessary to commit to it, then the next step comes: planning out your podcast.

That's right, you can't just set up your computer and microphone right now on the table and begin talking away. Each podcast needs to be carefully planned out with a clear objective that the podcast will achieve. Initially, planning out your podcasts might take up more time than you initially wanted, but once you get into the swing of things and have a schedule set for when you'll be making a new uploaded, you'll find that planning out each podcast will become incredibly easy and streamlined. If you want to, you can also set aside a few hours to plan out an entire month's worth of podcasts.

SHOW LENGTH

At the very least, you will want your podcast to be around 10 to 15 minutes. Some podcasts are up to a half hour to an hour in length, but since this is your first time it's a good idea to keep things simple. So for your first few podcast, aim for a minimum of 10 minutes and a maximum of 15 minutes.

OUTLINING YOUR SHOW

Keeping a 10 to 15 minute length in mind, the next thing to do is to write down an outline of your podcast. You can't have an outline of your podcast in mind. It needs to be written down either on paper or on a computer or tablet. Here's a good example of what the outline for your podcast should ideally look like:

Introductory Monologue: 1 Minute

Introductory Music: 30 Seconds

First Topic: 3 Minutes

Second Topic: 3 Minutes

Music Break: 30 Seconds

Third Topic: 3 Minutes

Fourth Topic: 3 Minutes

Conclusion Monologue: 1 Minute

Closing Music: 30 Seconds

You can change that outline as you see fit, but that's what it should basically look like. Always start with an introduction where you explain who you are and what your podcast is about, and then after the introductory theme song or music jingle, proceed to discuss between three to five separate topics that are all related to the niche of your podcast, with a 30 second music break midway through. Wrap up what you have covered in your conclusion monologue, which should be the same length as your introduction, and also mention what your next podcast will be about so listeners will already be looking forward to the next one.

RESEARCHING YOUR PODCAST

The next thing that you will need to do in planning out your podcast will be to write a script, but you can't write a script without first researching it. Research every single part of your podcast to make sure that your information is relevant and up-to-date. If you include bad information in your podcast and people find out about it, it would permanently damage your reputation as a podcaster. Don't let that happen and carefully research the topics for your podcast, writing down the most important or fascinating information that you will want to include.

WRITING THE SCRIPT

The next thing for you to do is to write out the full script for your podcast based on the results of the research that you have conducted. The script will obviously follow the same format as the outline that you wrote down before.

You want to sound as conversational as possible when people are listening to you on the podcast, so make sure that your script sounds conversational as well. Again, you will want to follow your outline. Start with an introduction where you explain who you are, a quick overview of what your podcast will cover, and why it helps the listener. You want to entice them to continue listening or watching. Since your introduction shouldn't last more than a minute, it should ideally not be more than five to seven sentences.

Your podcast will be divided into two segments with the 30 second music break separating the two segments. Between the two, the first segment needs to be the most interesting. If you've found information in your research that is particularly fascinating or little know, this is the place to include it in your script. Don't save it for later; otherwise people might become bored and not even get to it in the first place. Including the cool information sooner keeps their attention and will make it more likely for someone to listen through the entire podcast. Since each segment in our outline consists of two topics with each topic being about three minutes in length, you will want to make each three minute topic around two to three paragraphs, which translates to roughly four to six paragraphs per six minute segment.

In your conclusion, the first thing you need to do is thank your listeners for tuning in and ask them to subscribe to you if they haven't already. Offer a reward for subscribing if you can and to provide an additional incentive.

Very briefly summarize what you went over in the podcast and provide a couple of hints as to what will be covered next time. Finally, end the conclusion with your contact information so that people have a way to give you feedback and ideas.

Planning out your podcast is vitally important to your success as a podcaster. Never should you just plug in your microphone and start babbling away. To successfully plan out your podcast, determine the length of your show, write the outline for your podcast, research the information that you will include, and then write down a conversational, entertaining, and informative script that is based on the outline and utilizes your information while simultaneously being within the pre-determined length of your show.

Now obviously, not everything about your podcast is research or script based. A lot of is technically based too, and that's what we're going to be covering in the next step.

STEP 4: GATHERING YOUR EQUIPMENT

Since this is your first time as a podcaster, you'll want to keep things fairly simple. This means only using the essential equipment that you need, at least for now, such as: a computer, headphones, microphones, recording software, and speedy access to the Internet. Let's talk about each of these things in more detail:

COMPUTER

Your computer needs to be fast enough to handle typical recording for your podcast. Hopefully, the computer that you already have will be fast enough. You shouldn't have to go to the electronics store and buy a thousand dollar computer. In fact, the two or three year old $400 dollar PC Laptop you have should work well enough. But even if it doesn't, you can always buy a new model that has a faster processor and more memory.

HEADPHONES

You will need to have headphones if recording your voice with a microphone. This is because your speakers simply won't be able to be turned up loud enough to get rid of the feedback that the mike captures. However, headphones allow you to more closely pay attention to the quality of the sound that is being recorded.

Go with a pair of headphones that have a hard shell, constructed out of either rubber or plastic. Hard shell headphones are more effective for trapping the sound.

Remember that you get what you pay for with headphones. If you buy the cheapest pair of headphones on the shelf, even the cheapest pair of hard shell headphones, you're going to get the cheapest quality of sound. Maybe you don't mind that. But if you want your podcast to be of the highest quality, then you need good quality headphones at the very least. You don't have to buy the most expensive headphones on the shelf, but you definitely shouldn't buy the cheapest ones either.

MICROPHONES

Just as you get what you pay for with headphones, so you get what you pay for with microphones. The higher quality your microphones and headphones are, the more professional the sound of your podcast will be as well.

The best microphones are USB microphones. These kinds of microphones work the best with modern computers because they, as the name suggests, plug right in to the USB port on your computer and are therefore the most practical and the most versatile in today's era.

RECORDING SOFTWARE

You will need some sort of recording software to edit the audio of your podcast. You only really need a pair of headphones and a microphone to record your voice. But you also will need to mix your voice with other audio aspects of your podcast, such as the music. You need recording/mixing software in order to accomplish this, but the result will be that your podcast seems more polished and reputable. We'll talk more about editing audio later.

INTERNET

You have to have internet access because you have to have a way to upload your completed podcast online. If you don't have good quality or fast enough internet access at home, then go to a place in town such a coffee shop that does when the time comes to upload your podcast for the world to see (or hear).

STEP 5: MAKING THE PODCAST

By this point, you've accomplished a lot. You know fully why you want to start your own podcast, you have planned out every aspect of it, and you have gathered all of the required equipment that you need. Now the fun part comes: making the podcast!

In this step, we will run down the different parts of making your own podcast:

FINALIZE YOUR SCRIPT

Before you begin to record any sound, finalize your script. Read it over again to check for any spelling/grammatical mistakes and any changes that you want to make. If you have anybody available who is willing to read it, have them do so. They'll be able to catch things that you weren't able to, and they'll also be able to make suggestions for how you can make it better.

Once you have finalized your script and determined that it's enjoyable to listen to and contains all of the information that you want to share for this particular podcast, and have confirmed that your audio equipment is all functioning and working properly, the next thing to do is to record it.

RECORDING YOUR VOICE

This is arguably the most important part of the entire podcast production process. Your voice determines everything because it determines whether or not people will enjoy your podcast. Will you sound conversational or stand-off-ish? Will you be able to effectively articulate what you have written down in your script? Will you speak at a consistent audio level or will your voice get louder and then quieter? Will your voice be monotone or will it be passionate?

You should read your script as you go along, but you don't want to sound as if you are reading it. You also don't have to follow the script verbatim. Make a few improvs here and there as you go along, but stick to your outline at the very minimum.

Once you have completed your audio or at least a certain section of it, listen to the whole thing. Never proceed with uploading your audio without first listening to it. If you decide it needs work, then re-record it. At first, you may find yourself re-recording and re-recording your voice until you get it right. But after you've completed your first few podcasts, the recording aspect will become rather seamless.

Again, if you have anybody willing to listen to your podcast first, have them do so. They can make suggestions in regards to the volume of your voice, the inflection or enunciation that you put into certain words, and whether you sound like you're just reading a rigid script or having fun.

SAVING THE AUDIO FILE

Once you have completed recording your voice, the next thing to do is to save it to your computer. Always save it in an MP3 file format with a bit rate of 192 Kbps at the least.

Tag the file and give it identification information, such as your name (the artist) and an album cover or album art if you have any. If you do use album art, it needs to be free or non-copyrighted if it's online, or otherwise something that you have created yourself.

When naming your audio file, the file name must contain two things: the name of your podcast and the date (day, month, and year) of the episode.

That's it for actually making your podcast. Pretty simple, right? Finalize your script and check your equipment, record your voice, and then save the audio file. Yes, it really is that simple. Obviously you may need to re-record parts of your voice after listening to it, but again it will become more seamless with each podcast you make and the more comfortable you become with it.

But it's not time to upload your podcast and share it with the world yet. Yes, you have your audio file, but before you can upload it you next need to edit it. That's exactly what we'll be covering in the next chapter.

STEP 6: HOW TO EDIT YOUR PODCAST

There are some podcasters who upload their shows with very minimal to no editing. Therefore, you may decide for yourself that editing is not needed other than for some small trimming of audio in the beginning and the end. You may also decide that you don't need any complicated editing programs.

Here's the truth: editing audio can be a pain and is very time consuming, but it is necessary. You have to listen to your entire podcast episode and determine if there are any sections at all that need to be edited out. For example, where there any instances of you saying "um" or "uh" repeatedly? Did you ever get up and leave to go grab a glass of water or a soda? Is there an awkward long pause?

These are the kinds of things that you need to edit out of your podcast in order to make it look more professional. The kinds of people who don't put much work into editing their podcasts are either people who aren't very successful with podcasting because their audio does not sound professional, or those who have been podcasting exclusively for years to the point that they never stumble over words or make long pauses. Since you're likely neither of these people, you have to put the work into editing your podcast after you save the file.

MARKING POINTS TO EDIT

Rather than editing your podcast as you go along, listen to the whole thing at once and then mark the different points that you would like to edit. These marks are referred to as 'editing points.'

Examples of editing points include 'ums' and 'uhs,' loud background noise, long pauses, cross talking, an interruption, stammering over a hard to pronounce word, making an audible correction, and so on.

Marking editing points is easier than you think. Multiple recording apps and audio editing software that are available out on the market allow you to actually set a visible marker on the mark that you would like to edit.

MAKE EDITING EASIER WHEN YOU RECORD YOUR VOICE

What we mean by this is to give yourself enough margin while you're recording your voice in order to make editing easier. For example, it's much easier to edit out a three second clip of audio than a half second. So if you stumble over a hard to pronounce word, for example, immediately cease talking and be silent for at least three seconds, and then attempt the word again. That way, when you go to edit, it will be easier to edit out the part where you stumbled and the three second pause together than just the part where you stumbled alone.

PAY ATTENTION TO TRANSITIONS

The easiest points to edit on an audio file will be the transitions, especially if there are two or more people talking in the podcast. Examples include where one person has quit talking and another person has started talking. There can be some awkward silences or mistakes in between those two times, a prime riding point.

Also pay attention to the beginning and end of the transitions. You don't just want to edit out the middle parts. You also want to get rid of the beginning and end of the transitions in order for the audio to flow more smoothly and seem more natural.

PLAY THE AUDIO AT A FASTER SPEED

This may not sound like a wise idea, but most audio editing programs allow you to playback the audio at an increased speed. You won't want to increase the speed of the audio for the finished product for obvious reasons, but you should consider increasing the speed of the audio now and then and listen through it for areas of mistakes.

ONLY REDUCE SILENCES AND PAUSES; NEVER ERASE THEM

If there's a moment of silence or pause in your podcast, never edit out the entire pause. Instead, only edit out the beginnings and ends of that pause and then leave the middle in there. A little pause can sound natural; it's only when that pause is extended that it becomes awkward. Completely eliminating all silences in your podcast can make your voice sound robotic and things can also seem rushed as a whole.

Step 7: Publishing and hosting Your Podcast

Once your podcast has been recorded and edited, the next step is to publish it online so that people can access it. Let's assume that you would like to publish and host your own podcast on your blog or website. Here are the individual steps that you would need to follow in order:

HAVE AN AUDIO PLAYER INSTALLED ON YOUR BLOG

Without an audio player, your audience will be unable to listen to your podcast directly from your blog. You should be able to type audio player in the search plugins field in the plugins sections in the WP back office. You can then install your audio player directly from there to activate the plugin so audiences can listen to it.

CONNECT iTUNES TO YOUR BLOG

It's always a wise idea to connect iTunes to your blog if you want to maximize exposure for your podcast. You can accomplish this via FeedBurner. Simply post your podcast feed URL at FeedBurner.com, and select that you are a podcaster. Name your Feed Title and Feed Address. When the FeedBurner feed is live, the podcast will configure so that it can direct iTunes regarding where your podcast is on the internet.

That's really how simple it is for publishing your podcast. As long as you have a blog with an audio player installed and manage to connect iTunes to your blog and to your podcast specifically, you'll be able to have your podcast up on the internet for anyone and everyone to listen to.

However, you should never simply leave your podcast here as it is. If you do so, then the chances of it becoming popular are extremely narrow. You need to submit your podcast to other popular channels to increase exposure for it, to use certain techniques when you begin marketing your podcast to the world, and then you need to ensure that your podcasts remain popular over the course of time. That's what the remaining steps of this e-book will cover.

STEP 8: SUBMITTING YOUR PODCAST TO POPULAR CHANNELS

Never feel afraid to submit your podcast to publishers, hosts, and various podcasting platforms and channels. The truth is that most publishers and platforms will be very eager to accept your podcast. The reason why is because they have found out how to effectively distribute podcasts and then monetize them to make money, such as via in-app purchases and pre-roll ads.

For example, there are currently over a billion subscriptions to iTunes podcasts, and that number continues to grow. Nearly one fifth of all adults in the United States have reported listening to a podcast at least once, a figure which also continues to grow. If you want to take advantage of this awesome opportunity, then submitting your podcast to different channels is a must.

HOSTING SERVICES

There a number of different hosting services that you can choose from to set up your podcast. Examples include services that generate RSS Feeds automatically. Popular examples included LibSyn, TypePad, and Wordpress. However, these kinds of services for hosting your podcast will drastically limit how visible your podcast will be when people search for topics related to it. The reason why is because these hosts will insert their domain into your podcast information rather than your information, which limits your exposure. Nonetheless, it's a quick and easy place to start.

Other sites are available that are not built in with their own distribution service, and while you can certainly use these places to host your podcast, you will need to set up your own RSS (Really Simple Syndication) feed. This permits your content to be made available for other places to publish and distribute your podcast, and will also alert you for when those sites have updated their content with any of your podcasts or other forms of content.

In order to make this possible, simply submit the link to your RSS feed when you also submit your podcast to the website without their own distribution service. You may also want to consider submitting your contact information as well.

OTHER DISTRIBUTORS

By way and large, your best bet for submitting your podcast is going to be iTunes. Like we mentioned above, there are currently over one billion different subscriptions to podcasts on iTunes. This doesn't necessarily mean that there are one billion different people who have subscribed to podcasts, but still, a billion subscriptions is a number to be reckoned with.

One reason why iTunes is so effective as a podcast distributor is because it automatically reaches everyone who has an iOS device. And if you include iTunes tags in your XML file when you submit your podcast to iTunes, your podcast will be listed under the featured section and be more readily found by people surfing for podcasts in their areas of interest. Anyone who has downloaded a podcast app via iTunes will have even greater access to your podcast and may find it without even looking for it.

The best podcasting apps for expanding the visibility of your podcast will be Instacast 5 and Overcast. You'll still have to set up your RSS feed to have your podcast in these places, but that's not difficult.

Last but not least, consider making your podcast more widely available with a Creative Commons License. While it likely won't make a difference to the largest publishers, there's no harm done in allowing people to use your podcast and the content within it in the ways that you set down in the commons license. The podcast will still be fully attributed to you, and if anything, it may only increase your reach to potential new listeners and subscribers.

STEP 9: ANNOUNCING YOUR PODCAST TO THE WORLD

As a whole, podcasting is easier today than it ever has been in the past. With basic equipment that you likely already have at home and an enthusiasm to share with the world about what you know, it's very simple and straightforward to setting up an effective podcast.

However, setting up and then publishing the podcast is only part of the equation towards becoming a successful podcaster. It doesn't matter if you have the greatest podcast in the world; if nobody knows about it, then it's simply not going to get noticed.

That's why when you first publish your podcast, you need to do so with a bang. It's very unlikely that someone will take notice of your podcast and then spread the word. In other words, listeners and subscribers won't come to you. You need to go to them and find an audience yourself.

While finding audience members may sound like a challenging or daunting task, just remember that your podcast is high quality enough to attract an audience in the first place. You have fans already; they just haven't found you yet. You created a podcast that has excellent production value with the right equipment and you have informative and engaging content. You're only one step away from becoming a successful and highly regarded podcaster. So let's cover some different tips to gain notice for your podcast right off the bat:

GET YOUR PODCAST LISTED ON iTUNES

Yes, we've covered this one extensively already, but it simply cannot be stated enough. ITunes is one of the best places for any podcast to get noticed, especially considering that there are over one billion subscriptions to different podcasts on it already.

What's more is that you will find a step-by-step guide for publishing a podcast on iTunes, which further streamlines the process.

CREATE CAPTIVATING COVER ART

Sometimes it's not the name or subject of a podcast that gets it noticed, but rather the cover art that's on the outside. People will make a quick decision to buy or download your podcast if your cover art looks interesting, attractive, unique, or a combination of those things. It can ultimately be the vital difference between whether or not a person will become a subscriber. What's more, is that making your cover art look attractive and professional doesn't mean that you have to spend a lot of money. On some websites, it's possible to get a custom cover art design for only five dollars.

WRITE AN EYEBALL GRABBING DESCRIPTION

While everybody is going to notice your cover art first, the next thing that they'll be looking for before deciding whether or not to download your podcast is the description of it. That's why the description of your podcast that you write needs to be as equally attractive and appealing sounding as your cover art.

Different things that you should include in your podcast include what it's about, how it will help the listeners, the media format of the podcast, and how often you upload a new episode. Your description also needs to show your personality. It cannot sound dull or robotic in any sense of the words. Even if people like your cover art, if your description of your podcast fails to grab their attention or fails to make it sound like that your podcast will help them, they more than likely won't download it.

THINK HARD ABOUT YOUR TITLE

The other thing that you need to carefully think about is the actual title of your podcast. It can take days if not weeks while agonizing over what a good tile for your podcast is, and you will likely evolve your title and change it multiple times before finally settling on one.

Here's the best piece of advice that can be given to you in coming up with a title for your podcast: make it simple.

No, it doesn't have to be catchy, it doesn't have to be unique, it doesn't have to be artsy (even though all three of those things would certainly help). It just needs to be simple. No more than three words at most It needs to be to the point and clearly connected to the topic of your podcast so that when someone sees that title they'll say, "oh, so this podcast must be about..." And they should be able to say that just by your title alone, cover art and podcast description aside.

A two or three word title for your podcast is best. Consider using words that rhyme or words that begin with the same letter so that the title is more smooth when you say it.

To help brainstorm coming up with a title for your podcast, peruse around some other popular podcasts on iTunes and look for any patterns that you see in the titles for those podcasts. Do any of the titles rhyme? Do they use alliteration? Are they to the point? Are they memorable? Are they obscure? Are they connected to another form of media? These are just a handful of the different questions that you should ask yourself when brainstorming a title for your podcast.

ASK YOUR LISTENERS FOR REVIEWS ON YOUR PODCAST

One of the best ways to get your podcast noticed early on is to get positive reviews for it. You probably read online reviews of certain products or services everyday, or at least every week, from books to movies to hotels to technological equipment and so on. Podcasts are no exception. The more positive reviews you get for your podcast, both on iTunes and outside of iTunes, is guaranteed to increase the number of listeners and subscribers to your podcast.

Many of the most successful podcasters ask their listeners to leave reviews of the podcast on iTunes if they enjoyed it. You should do the same if you want to get your podcast noticed.

SET UP YOUR OWN WEBSITE OR BLOG FOR YOUR PODCAST

We touched on this one earlier in the form of blogs as well. It's incredibly cheap and simple to set up a site or blog for your podcast, such as via WordPress. What's more, is that sites like

WordPress allow you to directly interact with those who leave comments for your podcast as well.

Having a website or a blog for your podcast simply increases your credibility and will make it more likely for people to want to listen or subscribe to you. Be sure to leave a link to your website in the description for your podcast and mention it in your concluding remarks in the podcast itself.

STEP 10: GROWING YOUR PODCASTING BRAND INTO THE FUTURE

If you manage to gain initial attention for your podcast early on and find your listeners and subscriber base growing, then you've done a good job so far and you should congratulate yourself. However, there's one more thing that you have to ensure, that you continue to grow your podcast brand in the future and not only maintain the subscribers and listeners that you have gained so far, but make new ones into the future as well.

Here are some tips for how you can keep your podcast listenership and subscriber base steady and continue to bring in more people over the coming years:

AVOID MAKING WEAK CONTENT

"Don't make weak content? Got it!" This tip of advice may sound incredibly generic and clichéd, but it still needs to be mentioned, because there are many different ways that your content can be weak: it could be in a niche or field that is already covered by many other podcasts and therefore your own content doesn't stand out, it could not be unique or seem to rehashed from other people's podcasts, you may not have enough inflection or passion in your voice, you may be putting out information out there that a lot of people know already, your audio may not be of the highest quality, and so on.

There are a variety of different ways in that your content can be weak. That's why your podcast needs to be high quality all the way around.

AVOID PRESENTING YOUR CONTENT POORLY

Sometimes the problem with podcasts isn't that the information or content contained within the podcast is bad, but rather that it's presented in a poor manner. You can have the best content possible for your podcast, but if your presentation is a bust, then a lot of people are just going to tune out.

The best way to present content is to do so in a logical way that is easy to understand, and also in a way that keeps people engaged and wanting to come back for more because they think that your content will help them.

You need to communicate as clearly and as effectively as you possibly can, and you also need to make sure that your production value is top notch. You don't want any of these things to turn people away from the otherwise great information that you have to share with them.

ENCOURAGE YOUR LISTENERS TO INTERACT WITH YOU

If you don't encourage your listeners to interact with you, then you're making a fatal mistake for the long term. You want your listeners, particularly your regular listeners, to feel that you are a friend to them and the best way to feel like a friend is to engage and interact with them.

The good news is that there are many different ways to interact with your listeners: you can set up an answering machine to answer questions from listeners via the phone, you can engage with your listeners on the comments sections on social media sites such as Facebook, Twitter, or Reddit, you can hold contests and prizes for your listeners, and so on.

All of these techniques are critical ways to enhance the bond that exists between you and listeners of your podcast, and it also gives you an insight into what your audience desires so that you can incorporate that into your next episodes.

DON'T EXPECT EVERYONE TO FIND YOU

In fact, you should expect no one to find you or your podcast. Never assume that people will come to you just because you built something. That's literally the worst piece of advice that you could receive for just about anything.

Instead, actively market your podcast over the long term. A cool cover art or compelling descriptions and titles is only part of the equation. You also have to actively put your podcast out there so that it gets noticed by people who otherwise wouldn't have noticed it. Examples include submitting your podcast to blogs that cover the same sites and see if they will recommend or link to your podcast.

Continuously promote yourself and your brand over the long term. Only then will you be able to experience long term success vs. just short term success.

CONCLUSION

Thank you for reading this e-book! Podcasts truly do give you some of the best opportunities for sharing your knowledge and your creativity with the rest of the world, because it's extremely affordable, extremely easy, and enables you to reach out to a wide audience all over the globe.

In this e-book, we have learned everything from defining what a podcast is and the different reasons for why you would want to start a podcast, to how to plan out and create your podcast, to editing and uploading your completed podcast, and how to successfully market your podcasting brand to your target audience and ensuring that you continue to draw more people in in the future.

While podcasting is simple, it isn't easy. Each episode of your podcast needs to be carefully planned out, your voice recorded just right, and the editing nearly flawless in order for you to have a chance at attracting a large enough audience.

But if you are able to accomplish those things, you'll be able to unlock the many rewards that come with being a successful podcaster. You'll have full control over your content, you'll be able to forge a powerful relationship with your subscribers and your audience (and create an entirely new online community with them), distribute your content across the entire world, and be able to share your creativity and your knowledge in a way that does not need visuals like videos do.

Podcasts are one of the best ways in today's post-modern era for distribution of content and gaining a following. Since many people are stuck within the scheduled routines of their day-to-day lives, podcasts offer you a way to get your information to these busy people because they can tune into your podcast whenever and where ever they want. This is largely the reason why podcasts have become as successful and as popular as they have. It's also why more and more people have been turning to podcasting, which is likely why you first picked up this e-book as well.

As long as you closely take to heart the steps that we have outlined and explained for you, it will only be a short matter of time before you become a successful podcaster and unlock those benefits of podcasting that we've just discussed.

THANK YOU!

If this booked help you, then please share your
thoughts by leaving a review on Amazon

Made in the USA
Middletown, DE
29 December 2016